THE RED STAR DIARY OF 1916

Rena Corey and Bill Noxon

I hope you enjoy Bill's story.

Warmest regards,

Rena Corey

DEDICATION

To Louise Annette and Jessica Edwina--
the phenomenal women who are my
children and my friends.

ACKNOWLEDGMENTS

There would be no book about Bill without the work of James A. Nelson, Historian of the Town of Monroe, in Orange County, NY. Jim is an ace researcher and an enthusiastic and generous friend. He has provided many of the images of Monroe and has been with me every step of the way in producing this story. Thanks as well to Jim's friend, James Sweeney, Esq., who explored the diary's geographical descriptions and pinpointed the land and the identity of Bill's family.

Through the years, Stuyvesant High School unreservedly permitted the exploration of basement archives, year books and other materials.

Fr. Peter Schineller, S.J., Archivist of the New York Province of the Society of Jesus, generously allowed us to explore the wealth of information on Father Walsh and Monroe and unearthed Aunt Mamie's letter.

My daughter, Jessica E. Daley, always believed in Bill's story and drove me to finally tell it.

Almost all the photographs used are in the public domain, most culled from

The Library of Congress. Special thanks are owed to Jerry Fabris, Museum Curator of the Thomas Edison National Historical Park in West Orange, New Jersey, for the image of the Edison disc which Bill heard played at Stuyvesant.

My gratitude to the staff at St. Anastasia's Church, who sent wonderful material delineating the history of the churches in Harriman, Arden and Monroe.

And I am delighted, at last, to publicly thank my Samuel J. Tilden High School Social Studies teacher, Dr. Jules Kolodny, who instilled in me a respect for meticulous research which has guided my academic and professional life.

FOREWORD

The Red Star Diary of 1916 was purchased at a Maybrook, New York flea market in the summer of 1993. Lying on a blanket with an assortment of other merchandise, its purchase price of $1.00 was pre-set and I felt I had little to lose as I tucked the volume in my bag. Perhaps it would prove to be something I could add to my inventory and sell in the near future. As it turned out, this was the only diary I kept and would not offer for sale during my 28 years in business.

A sophomore at New York City's Stuyvesant High School, the writer spent his winter in Manhattan and his summer in Orange County. A fluid story teller, he packed a lot into each day's record. I was swept into his school life, farm life, relatives, religious fervor and his love of country, entertainments and baseball. He was philosophical; at times, deeply so. He was very funny, but not intentionally and – he was unidentified.

There was but one clue. On July 6, 1916, he quoted a reference to himself: "Bill."

As an antiquarian document dealer, I had sold thousands of letters, ledgers, journals and diaries and not once had I ever failed to identify the writer. And so began a twenty year quest to solve a mystery.

In that pre-home computer time, at least for me, one of the first people to whom I turned was the historian of the Town of Monroe, James A. Nelson. We worked together and separately, on and off through the years, combing the records at Stuyvesant; driving Monroe's country roads; scanning microfilm at New York's Municipal Building; reading old newspapers; hauling huge tax books from the shelves of the Orange County Clerk's office and then, of course, spending untold hours in cyber space. It was Jim, through his perseverance and with the assistance of his friend, James Sweeney of Monroe, who finally gave Bill his full name, William Gabriel Noxon.

In presenting Bill's life through his diary, I have been circumspect in not putting words into his mouth. As his voice after death, narrated events correspond to his experiences and have been carefully researched; photographs are of places he would have seen in his life time (e.g. nothing photographed after July 5, 1928 appears and whenever possible, 1916 images were used). Almost all illustrative materials are in the public domain.

In some respect, this work is fictionalized in that the central figure is dead, yet communicating with us. But I have looked at it as a textual documentary, ultra-illustrated and entirely factual.

There are no chapters, as I wanted the work to mimic the diary, flowing from day to day, although not chronological. The division lies between his life in the city and his experiences in the country, giving us a complete and vibrant feel for the urban and rural New York of 1916. There are central themes encompassing the military, commerce, religion, sports, politics, etc.

This is an often remarkable commentary by a Stuyvesant High School sophomore who leads us from the landmarks of New York City to the land of upstate farms. From Macy's to milk wars, from military maneuvers to the movies, Bill illuminates an intense relationship between city and country.

Fortified by a devout Catholicism and one of the boys influenced by the legendary Father Walsh, he struggles not only with his school work but with universal questions of flesh and spirit and the mysteries of death. Above all, Bill is an eye witness: a reporter who records the scenes of a distant, yet familiar, New York City and a rural New York, which has all but vanished.

The Red Star Diary of 1916 is a New York story colored by national events, from Pancho Villa crossing the U.S. border to World War I and the election of Woodrow Wilson. But ultimately, it is the story of a boy.

Publisher's note: This book quotes heavily directly from Bill Noxon's diary. These quotes are interspersed with Rena Corey's additions to tell the whole story. That which is a direct quote will be in standard text. *That which is added by Ms. Corey will be in italics.* Furthermore, since Bill's words are direct quotes, they will appear as he wrote them: unedited. While his English was remarkable for a high school student, there are occasional language and spelling errors which have purposely not been corrected.

The Red Star Diary of 1916

Wednesday, July 5, 1916: This is the day of death. Joe is slowly dying and will not last the night out. He has had every advantage to prepare. Fr Walsh has granted his two Plenary Indulgences. He came in at about 6:00 & gave him absolution. All day long Joe has been groaning. I did not see him. It will be good for Joe if he dies for he will never be able to get around again.

Thursday, July 6, 1916: Joe is dead. He died last night at 11:00. He did not say anything but tried to pray. He gave a little scream & then his breath grew shorter & he expired like one going to sleep. All this I heard this morning. The last words I heard of him were last Friday when he said on noticing my long pants," so you let them down, Bill."

He had all the advantages of a pious death that Fr. Walsh could do. The undertaker was up & I guess he will be taken away tonight. It is good May isn't up. I cannot feel sorry for I think that Joe died a good death

.

Saturday, July 8, 1916: Joe was buried this morning leaving the house at about 9: 15 for Arden. Everybody went except May. There was a horse hearse & two automobiles. Some boys from the Mt. House acted as pall bearers. They were too late in arriving and the mass was already finished. It was too bad.

Last night, the Ulfelder place burnt down. At about twelve o'clock I was awakened & after taking pictures of the huge blaze from our place went up. It was about burned down. May and Florrie passed there early in the night & noticed smoke curling from the chimney but paid no attention. It must have burned from 11:00 P.M. It was in complete ruins. Today I took two pictures of the ruins. It is believed that the wallpaperers left a cigar burning which gradually set fire.

It was also a July 5th when I realized that I was going to die from my struggle with tuberculosis. I had thought Joe so terribly young to leave us at thirty-nine, but I was only twenty-eight, as my birthday would not fall until November 11th. I was pleased that I would leave while up in Monroe, knowing that I would be lying in the Arden cemetery forever; that I would be joining my mother and that, eventually, my father and sisters and Aunt Mamie would be there too. Not that I hadn't loved New York, my days at Stuyvesant, and of course, baseball in the city streets. But it was my summer life in

4

the country that brought all of the family together and that's where we would remain, near the land that had been ours since the 19th century. I recalled that fire the night before Joe's burial and thought how much tragedy had visited us in a short period of time.

My own funeral, on July 9th, was at St. Anastasia's in Harriman, built in 1899, the very year in which I was born. Fitting, I thought, and hoped the beautiful little white church would have a much longer life than my own.

That year of Joe's death was so much in my memory because that was the year I kept a diary. And although they say that when you are about to die your life flashes before your eyes, in my case I slowly turned the pages of the days of 1916.

My mother was a Griffith and it was her family that was most prominent in my life. Her sister, Mary, or Aunt Mamie as we called her, ran the farm along with Joe, who had been adopted by my grandfather, James Griffith. My father, Henry Noxon, although a good man, had a serious drinking problem. Employed as a waiter in a New York City club, we were often concerned about him holding on to his job. Not surprisingly, I remember writing on the very first day of the year that Papa did not come home in the afternoon. We telephoned the club and found that he had left there at 6:30 PM. He came home at 10: 30, a little drunk. <u>Bad start</u> for the new year. The year ended in the same vein. At the beginning of December, I noted that we had bushels of trouble today. Papa came home last night with a black eye and drunk. He did not know how he got it but I believe somebody hit him. He has been drinking too much of late. I wish I were a little older to do something. But the real trouble was that he went to telephone the club that he wasn't going to work and instead went to work. I thought he most likely went to work but Mama worried all day.

And on Christmas, Papa was drunk. My mother worried all the next day about Papa's job but everything turned out all right.

Overshadowing Papa's unfortunate addiction in that first week of January was the much anticipated arrival of Mama's brother, Tom. He had not seen his sisters for 18 years, having gone out west to Winona County, Minnesota. We expected him to visit us in the city and then go on to Monroe, to the farm and

*Aunt Mamie. Of course, a lot had been
said about him. That he owned* 500 head
of cattle and 13 horses *made me sure that
he had* a very big farm and plenty of
money. *I imagined him* a tall man, *which
he was as well as thin. I observed* the
meeting between him and Mama was very
affectionate. He has a large moustache
which does not aid his appearance. He has
queer blue eyes. By what he says he
seems very rich. He praises his wife a
good deal.

*The Cedar Valley Stock Farm was,
in fact, his wife's property, over 260 acres,
won by a law suit from her relatives. Just
before my 9th birthday, she was savagely
gored by a bull that had been chasing a
dog that had been following her. Although
bleeding profusely from wounds in her
thigh and hip, and receiving delayed
medical assistance, my aunt Elizabeth
completely recovered.*

*By the 19th of January, Uncle Tom
had already met with the Assistant
District Attorney (whom he knew years
before and claimed he had aided), over
some property stolen from him. Perhaps
that's why he had returned to New York,
but that was unclear to me at the time.
John T. Dooling, the ADA, would later be
involved in high profile cases including oil*

7

stock swindlers and racketeers, Arnold Rothstein (who among many other things was reported to have fixed the 1919 World Series) and Nicky Arnstein. He himself was accused of wrong doing, seemingly in retaliation for his probes, but charges that had been leveled against him were eventually dropped.

My uncle fascinated me.

If Uncle Tom had that big moustache he wears shaven off he would look much better. It is a hindrance in eating. Uncle Tom is kind hearted and somewhat affectionate. Every time he meets someone he has not seen he stands up and surveys them intently & then says, 'I know you" or 'I'd never recognize you." He is a very stiff man and walks slowly and bent up somewhat. He is not so old either *(he was 56.)* I guess the hard work on his farm has affected him. It seems a characteristic in me to argument against anything anyone else says. I do this a great deal with Tom.

Uncle Tom talks a lot about the Guardians of Liberty or GOL's as he calls them. They put him off the school board because he is a Catholic. I guess they are very strong out there.

One of the nation's great military heroes, Lieutenant-General Nelson A.

Miles, was at the head of that anti-Catholic organization.

Lt.Gen. Nelson A. Miles
Brand Studios, 1898

If anything, I'd lived my life as a devout Catholic, as I reflected on February 12th:

I was in a somewhat melancholy state all day long occasioned by the fact that I intended to go to confession in the evening. I think during these fits of the emptiness of life, the results of sin and I have a firm conviction that a person who loves God and obeys his laws will have success in this life not withstanding that the good people seem to be in the direst straits.

Much of what I believed had been influenced by faithful attendance at St. Gabriel's Church on East 37th Street. Just two blocks from our apartment on East 35th, I attended services and played a lot of baseball in St. Gabriel's Park with the boys who attended the church school. Father Harris was a parish favorite and the congregation gave nearly $1000.00 to keep him when he was sick.

St. Gabriel's – 308 E. 37th Street

I had rocky times that year, fighting adolescent temptations of the flesh. Once, when I went to confession, I nearly was refused absolution on account of what I have already mentioned.

Monsignor Dunn spoke that February to the Knights of Columbus who were in the church after 7 o'clock Mass.

When I arrived at church it was pretty crowded although I was 15 minutes ahead of the time. First I went to the balcony but could not see well there so I took a side seat. I got a fine seat. The Monsignor was dressed in red. He was a fine speaker and talked smoothly and easily. He had a long face .He is pretty good looking. He talked chiefly about the Knights of Columbus and their work. Father Livingston introduced him. He was a beautiful speaker *and had attended St. Gabriel's parochial school as a boy.*

St. Gabriel's interior

John Joseph Dunn

The year of 1916, there was more than Uncle Tom's talking about anti-Catholic activities, and the Monsignor was right in the middle of it.

At that time, local government monies were given to Catholic charitable institutions and those of other faiths to care for New York City children in orphanages. When a new mayor, John Purroy Mitchel, was elected in 1913, he

13

appointed John A. Kingsbury as his Commissioner of Public Charities. It went downhill from there. Charges were hurled at the Catholic Church for keeping the orphanages in sub-standard conditions and worse. The Strong Commission was created. At this point, Father William B. Farrell wrote three pamphlets. One of them, published on February 16th, was entitled "A Public Scandal: Being an Analysis of Men and Motives Underlying the Investigations of the Charitable Institutions."

I was extremely upset by the daily headlines and news stories pointing fingers at the Church and their care of children.

There is a great deal about charity investigation now particularly against the Catholic places. Father Farrell was on the stand & in one of his pamphlets gives them a great laying out. Dramatic measures are needed. I suppose they think that each orphan should have a private valet.

I understood the depth and intent of the probe. The charity investigation is still going on & it is very prejudiced. They are after Father Farrell and his pamphlets.

14

By the summer, Father Farrell was the target of a police wiretap. Monsignor Dunn was charged with various crimes, including perjury and obstruction of justice. At the end of it, all charges against Father Farrell and Monsignor Dunn were dropped, but major changes were made in New York City concerning orphaned children.

NYC Mayor John Purroy Mitchel
City Hall – May 11, 1914

On March 5, at St. Gabriel's, I heard a lecture on the Venerable Oliver Plunkett by one of his descendants, Countess Plunkett, in the school hall. Oliver Plunkett died for the Faith & I guess he is to be canonized. It was a genuine Irish audience .When a picture of

Oliver Cromwell was shown many hissed but then burst out laughing. A   good deal of money was collected & the house was crowded.

The Countess' husband received his title in 1884. Created a Papal Count by Pope Leo XIII, he had donated money and property to the Sisters of the Little Company of Mary, a Roman Catholic nursing order. The Countess had given this lecture just the week before, in Brooklyn at St James Auditorium. The Brooklyn Daily Eagle *reported:*

> *The Countess will deliver an illustrated talk on 'The Life and Times of Archbishop Plunkett.' This lecture has been heard with much interest at the Catholic Club in Manhattan and in some of the parish halls in the borough across the river. There is no doubt that it will prove very enjoyable here. His Eminence Cardinal Logue and His Eminence Cardinal Farley have highly commended the Countess on the efforts being made to advance the cause of the beatification of the heroic Archbishop Plunkett. Those*

16

wishing to contribute to this worthy object may do so.

Oliver Plunkett
Beatified 1920

On April 24, the Countess' son, Joseph Mary Plunkett, as Commandant-General of the Dublin Brigade of Irish Volunteers, was one of the leaders of the

17

Easter Rising, which lasted until April 29th. He was a journalist and a poet and had suffered from tuberculosis from a young age. On May 4, 1916, he was executed by a firing squad at age 28.

POBLACHT NA H EIREANN.

THE PROVISIONAL GOVERNMENT
OF THE
IRISH REPUBLIC
TO THE PEOPLE OF IRELAND.

IRISHMEN AND IRISHWOMEN In the name of God and of the dead generations from which she receives her old tradition of nationhood, Ireland, through us, summons her children to her flag and strikes for her freedom.

Having organised and trained her manhood through her secret revolutionary organisation, the Irish Republican Brotherhood, and through her open military organisations, the Irish Volunteers and the Irish Citizen Army, having patiently perfected her discipline, having resolutely waited for the right moment to reveal itself, she now seizes that moment, and, supported by her exiled children in America and by gallant allies in Europe, but relying in the first on her own strength, she strikes in full confidence of victory.

We declare the right of the people of Ireland to the ownership of Ireland, and to the unfettered control of Irish destinies, to be sovereign and indefeasible. The long usurpation of that right by a foreign people and government has not extinguished the right, nor can it ever be extinguished except by the destruction of the Irish people. In every generation the Irish people have asserted their right to national freedom and sovereignty; six times during the past three hundred years they have asserted it in arms. Standing on that fundamental right and again asserting it in arms in the face of the world, we hereby proclaim the Irish Republic as a Sovereign Independent State, and we pledge our lives and the lives of our comrades-in-arms to the cause of its freedom, of its welfare, and of its exaltation among the nations.

The Irish Republic is entitled to, and hereby claims, the allegiance of every Irishman and Irishwoman. The Republic guarantees religious and civil liberty, equal rights and equal opportunities to all its citizens, and declares its resolve to pursue the happiness and prosperity of the whole nation and of all its parts, cherishing all the children of the nation equally, and oblivious of the differences carefully fostered by an alien government, which have divided a minority from the majority in the past.

Until our arms have brought the opportune moment for the establishment of a permanent National Government, representative of the whole people of Ireland and elected by the suffrages of all her men and women, the Provisional Government, hereby constituted, will administer the civil and military affairs of the Republic in trust for the people.

We place the cause of the Irish Republic under the protection of the Most High God, Whose blessing we invoke upon our arms, and we pray that no one who serves that cause will dishonour it by cowardice, inhumanity, or rapine. In this supreme hour the Irish nation must, by its valour and discipline and by the readiness of its children to sacrifice themselves for the common good, prove itself worthy of the august destiny to which it is called.

Signed on Behalf of the Provisional Government,

THOMAS J. CLARKE,
SEAN Mac DIARMADA,   THOMAS MacDONAGH,
P. H. PEARSE,   EAMONN CEANNT,
JAMES CONNOLLY.   JOSEPH PLUNKETT.

Proclamation of the Republic – Easter 1916

Joseph Mary Plunkett

Count and Countess Plunkett

Four days after their son Joseph's execution, the Count and Countess Plunkett were arrested. The Count was sentenced to 10 years penal servitude. His sentence was commuted and he was released in 1917. In 1921, a peace conference held in London was attended by Countess Plunkett. The conference resulted in the "Articles of Agreement for a Treaty Between Great Britain and Ireland."

I was also wrapped up in the subject of other major headlines: The Willard Moran fight.

I am very interested in the Willard Moran battle. I would like Moran to win. Willard is not a favorite with me. He thinks he is it. I always admired Moran .He fought Johnson when the black was in better condition than when he fought Willard. I expect a good battle. I went down to the Garden to see the crowds, At first I could not get near the building but once away could not get by the line of cops that were a block & a half from Garden. There were hundreds of them there. The crowds were great.

Arranging Madison Square Garden
for Willard–Moran – March 25, 1916

*Well, Willard won the fight in a
TKO, in front of 13,000 people, the biggest
crowd ever at Madison Square Garden,
and the most money the Garden had ever
made for one event: $152,000. George M.
Cohan was among the celebrities at
ringside. Even though there was some
debate about the decision, people were
saying that the film made of the fight
showed that Willard had won it. The
papers reported that the only reason
Willard didn't use his famous right hand
punch was because he broke his hand in
the second round. Two days later I was
fuming.*

I see that Mr. Hearst and ministers and rabbis are making a big fuss about the Willard Moran battle. Why don't they mind their own mission? Before the fight Hearst hired the best men to report it for him & praised it now after it is over he is against. He certainly is a many sided man.

The *World* denied the statement the Willard Moran fight was brutal by the *Journal* .I am glad to see that some paper protects the fighters. The *Journal* is always getting up something new. It has now a bunch of ministers writing their opinions on the fight. Half of them never even saw one. Of all nonsense this is the worst.

A month later I went down to see the Willard Moran pictures at the Palace. They were great. Moran is a game fighter. From the first round to the last he carried the fight to Willard. Every time Moran planted himself for a wallop Willard poked him with his long left & threw him off his balance. But in the seventh round Moran rocked Willard with blows & had him against the ropes. It seemed Moran won.

The Palace Theatre – 47th and Broadway

The Palace was a vaudeville theatre that featured headliners like Will Rogers, Ethel Barrymore and Lillian Russell. I had not been there before or after the Willard Moran showing.

Almost every Saturday, I went to see movies at the Regent. Located at Seventh Avenue and 116th Street in Harlem, the theatre seated over 2500 people and was very luxurious. Decorated in colors of red, blue and gold, with satin on the walls and deep blue carpeting, it featured a large mural above the stage. An orchestra accompanied the films and ushers took you to your seats.

Interior of the Regent Theatre
photo: Museum of the City of New York

I think I was a fair film critic. Helen Holmes was a major star from 1914-1917, playing a fearless daughter of a railroad president and performing all kinds of death defying stunts in the "Hazards of Helen." I paid 10 cents to see her in "The Girl and the Game" Episode 1, "Helen's Race with Death," and said, Never Again. Nothing extraordinary. *But I did go again and saw the last episode. This time* I liked the picture quite well.

On October 18th, a New York Times headline read, "'Daughter of the Gods' an Elaborate Amphibious Picture for the Submersible Star." They went on to write, "The beautiful figure of Annette Kellermann and her matchless skill as an amphibienne are made the most of," but they also said that it was a "somewhat monotonous photofable..." I concurred when I commented, Nothing much.

Annette Kellerman in *Daughter of the Gods*

The film I really liked was "Tillie's Punctured Romance" starring Marie Dressler, Charlie Chaplin and the Keystone Cops. I saw it three times, having seen it twice before in 1915.

Tillie's Punctured Romance – Marie Dressler and Charlie Chaplin

*Just the day before I saw "Tillie"
again,* Benny and I went to the circus. We
paid 75 cents & got a fair seat on the
Madison Avenue side. The show was not
so good as usually is. I missed the
Japanese wrestlers. The bears could skate
& ride a bicycle but their act was very
short. There were many of the old
features there. I like the trapeze
performers the best of all. There was a
girl in the freaks from Russia- a
Circassian. She was certainly beautiful
with a great mass of curled hair. There
was another man who must have been 9 ft.
His thumb could cover a dollar piece. He
was bigger than the cowboy. Besides the

sword swallower and fat people there was a man who was supposed to be turning into stone. That's a lie for his blood would stop circulating & he would die shortly after.

1916 Poster

The Skating Bears

There were many times I was exposed to more intellectual entertainment. In May, my sister Mary got two tickets for P. Yon's concert at Aeolian Hall. *Pietro Yon had come to the United States to fill the position of organist at St. Francis*

29

Xavier Church in Manhattan. The Vatican appointed him, "titular Organist," an honor no one had ever held before. In 1917, he and his brother, pianist S. Constantino Yon, and Metropolitan Opera star, Giovanni Martinelli, performed in Monroe to benefit the American Red Cross and Civilian Relief. Martinelli and Pietro Yon were close friends and both owned summer homes in Monroe.

Pietro later became the assistant organist for St. Patrick's Cathedral and was in charge of the dedication recital for the cathedral's new organ at the start of 1928. I lived to see him become music director for St. Patrick's. Perhaps I was not as good a music critic as a judge of movies:

It was good I suppose, for those who like that kind of music but I don't. They would play a few notes & then take 2 or 3 minutes rest. Marone played on the piano & was good. Another composition by Yoni was played on organ was fine, about the best.... I fell asleep a few times during the concert.

In May, we had a dandy assembly the best I ever remember. It was sort of an advertisement. A man from the Edison Company played about four selections on the new Diamond Disc. One was the "Ave Maria." It was truly beautiful & inspiring. Another was "She Lives Down in Our Alley," a 3rd "My Lady of the Telephone" & the fourth a march. They were a fine selection.

My Lady of the Telephone published Feb. 1915

One week later, Stuyvesant provided another terrific event. Ernest Thompson Seton, the author of "Wild

Animals I Have Known" spoke in the assembly. He spoke of totems and showed how trade marks descended from them. He is a good talker. He is very dark & looks like an Indian. He has a black moustache.

Ernest Thompson Seton

Tannerey, with his dogs, came galloping up the cañon.

A Drawing from *Wild Animals I Have Known* –
1898

    A couple of years after he spoke to us at Stuyvesant, he wrote "Sign Talk of the Cheyenne Indians and Other Cultures." Other languages and cultures intrigued

34

me. In April, we were given a very interesting lecture at assembly. A man talked of Japanese language & customs illustrated he could speak the language & showed how a few syllables were formed. For instance, this ⊖ signifies sun because it is round as the sun is. The 1st line indicates clouds. This 朩 indicates daylight. The sun is above & a tree which is mostly seen before the sun at the rising of the sun. It is certainly a queer language.

Stuyvesant, when I attended, was located at 345 East 15th Street, having moved from its original East 23rd Street location. Opening on September 9, 1907, the handsome Beaux Arts building, designed by Charles B.J. Snyder, Superintendent of School Buildings for the City of New York, fulfilled the educational concepts of William H. Maxwell, the first New York City Superintendent of Public Instruction. He had been the Superintendent of Schools in Brooklyn from 1887 to 1898, while that borough was still an independent city. Mr. Maxwell believed in the benefits of manual training. So, besides Latin, Geometry, English and Spanish, I was burdened with mechanical drawing, wood-turning and pattern making.

Stuyvesant High School – 345 East 15th Street

I was a good, but not stellar, student and always felt concerned at exam time and grateful when I pulled through.

Hurrah! I passed in all my subjects. Below is my marks. The first mark is the last month's mark and the last is the exam mark. The little figure is the term of the subject.

Latin 3   75-78
Geom 2 65-60
Eng. 3 70-75

36

Mec. Draw 3 64-88 Regents
Wood Turn 3 78-80
Gym 3- 80-80

I had a close shave in Geometry.
The exam mark in Mec. drawing is fine.
And I did not think I would get such good
marks in wood-turning either.

*When the last day of the semester
arrived on January 27th*, my standing in
my class was fifth place with 73%.Gleason
was the highest with 83%.To tell the truth
my last month's and exam's mark were
higher than I ever expected to receive and
I consider that I did good.

The whole class is promoted to the
morning session which begins at 8:00.

I had some confusion in getting
started on the new program. It was
however easy to follow after getting the
idea. I am with Fuldner and Friedman in
Spanish and Latin. I have Mr. Reynolds
in Latin. He recognized me immediately. I
am with Friedman in Geometry and with
Fuldner in pattern making. I shall not put
down my rooms yet until I am fully
settled. I had some job inducing Fuldner
to come to Mr. Reynolds rooms. He doesn't
seem to like him .Oakes the swimming

guy is in my class. Classes are no longer designated by letters.

My friend, Mansfield Fuldner, was two years younger than I but scheduled to graduate in June of 1918. His family lived on Fort Washington Avenue in Washington Heights and his father, Henry, worked for the Abraham & Straus department store in Brooklyn. Fuldner graduated from Princeton in 1922, and from the University of Virginia School of Law in 1926, where he was on the board of the Law Review. In 1927, he sailed on the Franconia for Australia.

Mansfield C. Fuldner, left,
at the Aerodrome, Essendon

*Oakes lived in the Bronx on East
179th Street. He was a couple of years
older than I and on the Stuyvesant
swimming team which, in 1913-1914, won
the Public Schools Athletic League
championship. Oakes graduated in June
of 1916.*

*The only sport that interested me in
school was baseball, and in April* I
volunteered for the class baseball team. *I
loved playing baseball, particularly as the
catcher. The spring months were filled
with street games in the neighborhood. On
May 21st: ...we* won our first game against

39

a good team. A muff on the catcher's part lost the game for them as a runner on third scored & it was the last half of the ninth. Curran's safe bunt helped to put the guy on 3rd and it was 2 out too. I got 2 hits. I hit a terrific foul. I did not think it was one & was easily good for a homer. I busted the cover on the ball. We had 2 new players. Meany & Mike from 36th St. They are pretty good fellows. In the first inning I nailed a guy on 2nd & nobody stole again. Gould pitched fine. A couple of fellows got 3 balls in succession & then Gould put 3 strikes over. He was a little rattled in the 9th.

Score 31st 0-1-1-2-1-0-0-0-0 = 5
35th 1-0-0-0-0-1-1-2-1 = 6

We won our game by a score of 28-8! Home score. We literally wiped the street with the opposing team. They were the Lincolns from 36th. Gould pitched. He got a home run & also Bon Joe & I. It was like pie beating them.

We had been looking for suits for the team for some time and found them at Macy's for $2.50 apiece. I bought one and, by the first week in June, we had seven.

40

Norman Rockwell – May, 1916

The last city game I played was on June 18th. It did not turn out well.

We lost our game 10-11! It was a badly played game. We were chased from field to field and had some job getting settled. Bon Joe practically lost the game. With a man on third he tries to steal third forcing the man out. There was only one out too. He let two bum batters up in the

41

last lick & they got put out. I made a nice homer sending a man in and sent 2 more men in by drives. Winberry cannot play. He is very slow and could not hit. He did, however, send two men in by bunts.

Baseball may have been over, but there was a lot of excitement in the streets the very next day.

From all over at night we could see the soldiers assembling at their respective armories. It was good to see them. Such a sight arouses patriotic feelings in everybody. It is also said there were a great number of volunteers. I would like to see the army enter Mexico & clean up. Things have been too free down there.

These maneuvers coincided with orders issued by the State Adjutant General's office, from the State Arsenal in New York City:

> *"In accordance with a proclamation of the President of the United States dated June 18, 1916, calling out under the Constitution and laws of the United States a part of the organized militia to be employed in the service of the United States, the Commanding General Division*

42

>*will cause the organization of his command, less coast artillery troops, to assemble forthwith at their respective home stations in the equipment prescribed for field duty preparatory to their muster into the service of the United States."*

The troops were going after Mexican revolutionary, Pancho Villa, who had kidnapped 18 Americans in January and then, in March, crossed the border at Columbus, New Mexico, torched the town and murdered 19 people. On June 21st, I went down in the morning at 8:30 to see the 69th off. I saw some come out of the armory & then I hurried up to the Cathedral to see them pass. Cardinal Farley was standing on the steps of the Cathedral to review them. As they passed they faced right saluting him, the officers, with their hands. There were some crowds about for a working day. The paper said a thousand went away. I love to see soldiers for it always raises a flush of patriotism in me. The next few days will determine war. I would like to see it.

Just the week before, we had General Wingate speaking to us at assembly when he presented the Wingate

43

Trophy to our school. He spoke on
military training and the weakness of the
arguments opposed to it. He said some
very interesting things and sensible too.
He served in the Civil War. A few other
speakers spoke on the advantages of
military training. One was a Captain and
the other a physical instructor.

Theodore Roosevelt with Gen. George Wood
Wingate to his left, taken at Central Park, at a
meeting of the Public Schools Athletic League.
1913

The 69th leaving for Mexico – June 21, 1916

Reviewing the 69th from St. Patrick's Cathedral –
June 21, 1916

The Evening World – June 21, 1916 –
Final Edition

On the 27th, I saw the 71st leave for the border at 11:30. It was a grand spectacle. The crowds were immense all along the course. I went to 42nd Street with them.

This was certainly the year of military events. Teddy Roosevelt started the Preparedness Movement, which campaigned for a strong American military after the outbreak of the war in Europe. At first, President Wilson opposed the idea, but after the sinking of the Lusitania in 1915 and Pancho Villa's raid

46

on Columbus, he changed his attitude. On May 13th, I went over to see the Preparedness Parade in the morning. It started at 9:30 from the Battery & marched to 59th St. It was great. It said there were 145,000 men in it. I believe more. ...A few fellows went over to see the parade at 8:30.It was fine at night .All militia & cavalry were in it. The cavalry were great. They galloped most of the time. The baggage mules were much in evidence. Many canon, guns etc. Preparedness will clean up on this monster parade.

The Sun *declared on May 21st:*

"GREATEST CIVIC PARADE IN NATION'S HISTORY VOICES NEW YORK'S DEMAND FOR PRE-PAREDNESS

New York's huge Preparedness Parade of last Saturday has passed into history as the greatest civic demonstration ever made. In point of numbers, in length of line and in duration it was exceeded only by the Grand Review of the Army of the Potomac in 1865. The metropolis has spoken and its voice is unmistakably on the side of adequate national defense."

Fifth Avenue decorated for the
Preparedness Parade

The Preparedness Parade
Municipal Building – Centre Street

Monroe

Postcard – Erie Railroad Train at Monroe c.1916

So much of our life on the farm depended upon the Erie Railroad. That's how we got to Monroe from Manhattan; how our boarders came up and returned to the city; and how we shipped our milk. Supplying New York City with pure Orange County milk was a huge industry and had been since the Erie first enabled the area farmers to do so in 1842.

Erie Railroad Train at the Monroe Station.
c.1916

Despite Joe's precarious condition, work at the farm went on.

I went with the milk this morning & met two trains. Some work for first day. Yesterday I also went with the milk. I have been going every day now since July 1 & am now well accustomed to it. We buy the ice cream now so I don't have to make it. It is a good thing since the freezer is no good now.

On July 12th, went with the milk again today. It is the last time I will go. I had a great deal of trouble with money orders & money. *But in August, I began taking the milk again every morning and on the weekend in September, when I came up from the city.*

Postcard – Horse and Cart at Monroe Station
c.1913

The last Sunday in September, I was aware that the farmers plan to strike today. Yesterday, Nobody took their milk.... I believe the farmers will eventually win out if they all hold together.

51

*Founded in Orange County in 1907,
The Dairymen's League of New York State
had 13,000 members whose herds totaled
190,000 cows in 1916. The League's
Executive Committee sent out impassioned
communications to the farmers urging
them to hold out for fair prices and not
give in to large dealers. "For sixty years,
you have sold milk to Bordens at their
price. Now is the time to shake off their
despotism and get a fair price for your
product." And although the committee
urged their members to be non-violent,
masked men held up milk wagons in
Herkimer County on the first of October.*

The New York Times *reported:*

"FARMERS CUT OFF CITY'S
MILK TODAY

Dealers Admit Three-fourths of
Up-State Supply Will Be
Stopped.

LEAGUE'S FIGHT ON
"TRUST"

Producers, Led by Dillon, Won't
Renew Oct. 1 Contracts, Except
Through Organization.

BABIES AND SICK FIRST

Deliveries Today and To-morrow -- New Sources Sought in Canada -- Prices Rise.

Because the farmers believe there is a milk trust in New York City, which is not fair to them, and because the milk dealers believe there is about to be created a farmers' trust which will hamper them, 75 percent of the city's milk supply will be cut off today."

By October 3rd, the milk strike was beginning to affect New York. I could get no milk this morning *but, by the 5th, it was all over. Papers throughout the city and state reported that the Borden Company, one of the "big three" dairy companies, had given in; the newspaper,* The Saratogian, *stated the primary concern was for the babies. The Dairymen's League had won.*

Papa came up the second week of July and Uncle Tom was there too. The three of us cultivated and hoed the beans. Up at the next place I cultivated & Pa led the horse. He also cultivated but did not

53

know how & dug up a number of beans.
We will have a nice big bean crop.

As a break from our chores, we went to Henry Brunner's place on Cromwell Lake.

Papa and I went fishing and stayed from 10: 30 to 3 o'clock .We caught 23 fish all perch except two sun fish. We had about 7 quite large perch. We got a boat but had no money to pay for it so Brunner said to let it go. We also borrowed poles from him. *At the end of the year, Mr. Brunner lost a long fight waged against him by the Commonwealth Water Company. The Appellate Court of the State of New York ruled he had no right to have people boat, fish or swim from his Lake View Hotel. He had been in business a long time.*

Courtesy Woodbury Historical Society

Men Fishing on Cromwell Lake
Courtesy Woodbury Historical Society

Our 75-acre farm had been deeded to my mother, Rose, and her sister, Mary, in 1890. Like Mr. Brunner and so many other residents of the area, we rented rooms during the summer. The Erie brought guests to Monroe and neighboring towns.

As far back as 1901, Aunt Mamie had been advertising the place. In 1906, a publication put out by the Erie Railroad, "Rural Summer Homes," showed M. Griffith's accommodations for 20 guests at $2-9 a week. Being 2 1/4 miles from the station was a plus.

The "M" and arrow tip pointing at the
Griffith farm
Atlas of Orange County – A.H. Muller – 1903

I met the trains and picked up the boarders.The 29th of July was a typical day. Two women & babies came up on the 11 o'clock train & Mr. Burns & his son came on the 4:46 & the Dennis girls came. We did not expect the girls & I don't know if they will stay or not. We thought we would have no people this summer & we have more than we ever had.

People came unexpectedly and stayed longer than anticipated. And there were squabbles. Miss Biber said the Aunt had a grudge against her. That she would miss nothing when she went home as she had a better bed, better food and better air(somebody she said told her about the air).I wonder why she stays at all if that is the case. We could easily get along without her as the place is crowded. *When she finally left, she had wanted to go* to every store in town but the breeching came loose & I gave that as an excuse *and left her at the hotel.* I am certainly glad she is gone.

Postcard – Monroe Main Street c.1908

My sister Mary and Aunt Mamie had a big argument as to where they will put the Byrnes. Three big men. The Aunt wants to put them all in one room while the Rosenbaums have one room a piece. She is even saving a room for May Rosenbaum. It certainly is a shame. For those rotten Jews she would do anything. She considers them so above her that she licks their feet. *Dr. Rosenbaum and his family were well-to-do and unlike the Jews described to us by my cousin Johnny, the tenement inspector.* He said that the condition of the Jews is awful. They sleep ten in a bed lying crossways. They dress well and live five families in five rooms and live on a loaf of bread. They eat fish and sometimes chicken when killed immediately. Johnny said they keep together a lot. They have no more brains than anyone else but do have initiative and nerve. This is exactly my opinion and I have learned by experience. *In May, at Stuyvesant, a* tenement house inspector talked about houses in New York, especially below 10th Street. He verified John's words about the sleeping and cleanliness of the Jews & Wops.

NYC tenement inspectors in basement living quarters

In April, on the way to school, there was a fellow giving out the "Call" a Socialist paper in opposition to military training. It made my blood boil & I felt disposed to beat up a couple of them. That's all that was discussed in school. Socialism. Nearly all Jews belonged to it. I had an argument with one Jew who thought he knew everything about it. Although I do confess I do not know much about Socialism I beat that fellow all to pieces in a few minutes. He would not argue at all. Another fellow was afraid to argue with me. I mean to draw up a list of objections against socialism.

As I had anticipated, Mrs. Silverman did not come up to board. Mr. Silverman had died very suddenly in May and I felt it was really too bad. Morton was just beginning to appreciate his father & the other kid was just beginning to be cute. Mr. Silverman loved Morton very much too. I don't suppose Mrs. S. will be in the country this summer. It seems he dropped dead from indigestion in his office. It is strange. In no ways does death give a perception of its coming. Its far reaching arms entwine without warning or mercy.

There was a lot of haying to do, as well as berry picking. Some days it was too wet to work and others so hot that I became very tired. On July 18th, it was clear & we put in a lot of hay; all in the orchard that was cut. Some around the house was too wet to put in. Uncle Tom came up but did nothing. He refuses to lift a hand but tells the ladies how it is done in Minnesota & what they use. He does not seem accustomed to lifting hay. One of the boarders helped a great deal.

Uncle Tom had strong opinions. In 1912, The Winona Republican Herald *wrote an article about his opposition to proposed concrete highways. He felt automobiles would frighten the horses, and because of this, the farmers would not be able to use the roads much. In fact, he advocated separate roads for each.*

Papa & I picked about 3 qts of huckleberries. In about five days there will be enough to sell. *The next day,* I took Papa down to meet the 8:31. He is going to send me a dollar & I am going to send him back the pictures I took of him. We worked all day in the hay.

The huckleberries seem all right to be picked about Monday. I am going to give Tillie Bull 2 qts free as an inducement. The next week I picked Tillie 10 qts I keep a record .I will not write down here what I sell. I saw a great big Pilot snake in the swamp & was within 3 inches of him. I had previously passed the same spot twice. I was all afternoon picking berries .They are not very ripe as yet. *The next* day there were no berries to be picked so I had a little rest raking up the hay on the side hill .I used the team. We have an awful lot of hay this year. The rest of that lot will fill Fred's barn & there already is some hay in the other barn. It will not take much more to fill that. Both bins up at the next place are nearly filled & there is yet a lot to get. But I suppose the more hay she has the more she'll give.

Haying with a team

Some things remained as they did in the city. I continued to play baseball, attend Mass and go to the movies.

A center for all three of these activities was the Seven Springs Mountain House Mission.

Postcard – Seven Springs Mountain House
Mission c.1916

Originally, the Mountain House was a luxurious hotel built on 70 acres by the Davison family in the 1860's. The hostelry accommodated 400 guests, among whom had been Ulysses S. Grant, Admiral Dewey and Horace Greeley. For a time, President Grant kept a suite of rooms there for himself and his cabinet officers. On July 3rd, 1874, so many people arrived at the Monroe Station that every horse and carriage for miles around was hired to pick up Mountain House visitors. By the afternoon, the hotel had been filled to capacity and 200 late arrivals were turned away to board the Erie and return to New York.

Seven Springs Mountain House after closure
c.1903

Eventually falling upon hard times, the hotel was purchased by the Jesuit Mission of Our Lady of Loretto, founded in 1891 on Elizabeth Street in New York City. Run by Father William H. Walsh, the parish served Italian immigrants and, as they were a poor group, Father Walsh used

65

the Mountain House as a summer camp for the boys of these families.

Father Walsh telling stories to the boys

Over the years, Father Walsh faced daunting events. On the night of July 4th, 1913, the four story frame dormitory at the Mountain House was consumed by fire. As the boys had been well trained through fire drills, they all escaped unharmed. Father Walsh then over saw the re-building, which was enabled in part by shipments of steel to Monroe on the Erie Railroad.

Boys' dormitory in ruins – July, 1913

Tents provided by George M. Cohan
after the fire

Four years earlier, The Monroe Gazette *reported that the Black Hand had threatened to blow up the Loretto church in New York unless Father Walsh paid $500.00 to their representatives.*

The New York Police Department sent detectives from the Italian Bureau to guard the 600 pupils at the church school. Many of the parishioners regularly paid extortion to these Sicilian mobsters.

Dynamite bomb planted by a Black Hander in the hallway of No. 356 East Thirteenth Street, New York City. *McClure's Magazine* (May 1912).

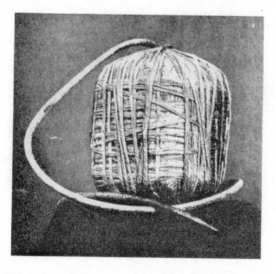

Father Walsh invited us to the moving pictures and we went. The picture shown was Our Lady of Lourdes in three parts & Columbus one part. The character of Bernadette in the former was not very well acted.

On a couple of occasions, I went to church in the village, but most Sundays I went to Mass at the Mountain House. Baseball often followed services. On September 3rd, we had two games of ball. The one in the morning was fine. It lasted 14 innings the final score being 9-8 favor us. In the last inning we made 4 runs & they 3 runs. In the afternoon the working boys lost to the college boys 15-8. I played with the working boys. There is some friction between the two I am not sure what it is all about.

Playing baseball at Seven Springs Mountain House-1912

The following Sunday, there were not enough fellows at the Mt. House to play ball so I walked over to see Homer. He is all developed but smaller than I am. He has a rotten job. Gets $30.00 a month & has to mind boats, run the auto, keep bar, beat a drum & minor jobs. He says he makes a lot of tips. He smokes & drinks. It is a bad place for a kid.

A week later, I learned he got a job in the repair shop ...paying $6.00 a week for board & lodging & gets $1.25 a day. Not bad at all for a beginner. *And better than the work gotten in May by* three boys on the block: Nino, Nick, & Dutch got jobs for $13.50, $12.00, $15.00 a week respectively in a bottle manufacturing place in Long Island. They went to work in the morning & could last but half a day it was so hot. Dutch fainted & was kicked out. He didn't get a cent. The others got a $1.00 apiece.

Gould had been in my gymnastics class. One day I took a walk with him to light the lamps. Believe me it is some job & he only gets $3.50 a week for it. He has to light 64 lamps & put them out at 2 o'clock in the morning .He has very little sleep.

Work was very important to me. One day I went to Central Park. The rich

70

men I saw walking along the street made me resolve to work and to become like them for Mama's sake to give her some comforts of life in her old age.

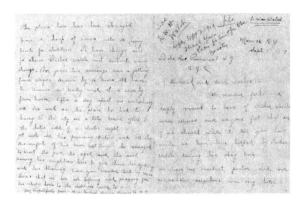

In 1919, Father Walsh became seriously ill. Aunt Mamie wrote to the Provincial Father in New York:

Monroe, NY
Sept 1, 1919

To the Rev Provincial S.J.
N.Y.C.

Reverend and dear Father:

We, Monroe folks, were deeply grieved to hear of Father Walsh's severe illness and everyone felt that one of us should write to tell you how much we have been helped by Father Walsh during his stay here.

We have no resident pastor and our non-Catholic neighbors were very bitter against the church and her priests. Father Walsh hired a contractor to build the children's summer house from a nearby town.

The people of this town were so bigoted it had been very difficult to even buy land to build a Catholic Church. The contractor himself was so bitter he would not use the title 'Father" in speaking of a priest.

During the progress of the work this man grew to think so highly of Father Walsh that after the work was finished he sought out the priest nearest his house and helped him in many ways. They have become fast friends and the man has declared his intention of becoming a Catholic.

He is one of the 'big men' of his town and of course this change in him has had its effect upon others. But this man is only one of the many Protestants of this little cluster of towns that grew to admire, respect, and love Father Walsh-a Jesuit priest.

Each one of us feels sorry to hear that he has been taken from this work where he has done so much at the cost of so much pain. The place here has been changed from a heap of ruins into a fairy land for children. To have things nice for them Father Walsh went without many things. For years his carriage was a jolting farm wagon drawn by a lame old horse; his dinner a hasty meal at a nearby farm house. After a day spent in overlooking all the work on the place he had to hurry to the city on a late train often in the bitter cold of a winter night.

Yet with all his pressing duties and all the discomforts of his own ill health, he managed to visit the poor, the aged, and the sick among his neighbors here to give them his sympathy and his blessing. Can you wonder that we miss him? that we are all hoping and praying for his return here to the children and to us?

Very respectfully yours,
Mary Griffith
Monroe, Orange County, N.Y.

From the beginning of the year and all through the summer, I had saved to purchase a typewriter. I visited the typewriter store on 23rd Street to price an Underwood and received offers in answer to my inquiries to the Typewriter Emporium. I wished I had the money to buy one on the installment plan. By mid-September, I had saved $28.25 and I got my typewriter. It is a Remington No 10 & a beaut. Two colored ribbon back space & a number of characters. It is a $35.00

machine but I got it for $28.00. It is a bargain as it writes fine.

Having my own machine enabled me to work from home after school and, in November, I placed an ad in The Evening Telegram. *It appeared right above the Lost and Found column:* TYPEWRITING--At home; first class; 5c page. WILLIAM NOXON, 213 East 35th St.

July flew by very fast. *On the 12th of August,* Frank Byrne & I went to Walton lake to see the swimming carnival but it was postponed to next week as we later learned. Nick met us in the village & carried us to the Lake. I don't like the place much. We were out rowing with the French girl & the younger one. She is a gay bird & speaks with an accent. Her name is Dumont. We walked all the way home.

Postcard – Walton Lake Inn c.1913

The following Saturday, I went down with Hubert to Walton Lake to see the races. The horse of Hubert's could certainly go & Hubert is a very reckless driver. He came very near having more than one collision. Homer came in second in the boat race for men. He went in the dive only on his nerve. The canoe tilting contests were fine. They were the best part of the fair. There was one good swimmer and diver there.

August 30th was the last recreational trip I made for the season. I went out riding with Hubert & May Rosenbaum .We drove to Walton Lake & we went swimming.

I don't know when to go back to school. I read that the high schools will not open until September 25. I would like to know when I can get my program straightened out.

Normally, I would have returned to Stuyvesant on September 11th and come back and forth on the weekends, but 1916 was not a typical year. In Brooklyn, on June 17th, official announcement was made of the existence of an epidemic of Infantile Paralysis. By the end of June, there were 646 cases in Kings County. We had come to Monroe, as was our custom, but thousands of people fled to the country to escape the disease.

People boarding the railroad to escape the polio epidemic – 1916

Because the first victims had been Italian children, there were thoughts that Italian immigrants had carried the disease to New York, but there had been no evidence of the disease in any town in Italy.

The New York Times *reported on July 10th that the departments of police and street cleaning and the Society for the Prevention of Cruelty to Animals were uniting with the Department of Health, the Rockefeller Institute and private doctors "in a city-wide fight against the spread of infantile paralysis." By then, 302 children had been attacked by the disease and 67 had died. At the end of the year, almost 9,000 cases had been reported in New York and over 2400 deaths.*

New York mother carries child to hospital
transport – 1916

FEARS PARALYSIS WILL FLARE AGAIN

August 20, 1916

Deputy Health Commissioner Sees Peril in Return of Children Now Away.

ALL PARENTS ARE WARNED

Believes Many, Before Unexposed, Will Get Disease on Coming to City.

SLIGHT INCREASE IN CASES

Day's New Victims Number Nine More Than on Friday—36 Die, Four More Than Day Before.

Record of the Disease in the City.			
	Deaths.		New Cases.
Borough	Fri- day.	Yester- day.	Fri- day.	Yester- day.
Manhattan	17	12	44	52
Brooklyn	6	13	48	45
Bronx		2	8	13
Queens	7	6	20	25
Richmond	3	1	5	..
Totals	32	36	125	134
Total of deaths to date			1,597
Total of cases to date			7,002

There was a slight advance in the number of new cases of infantile paralysis yesterday over the number on each of the several days preceding. The total of cases to date was carried above 7,900. Health Commissioner Emerson, however, saw no reason for discouragement, and was especially pleased with the continued evidence that the epidemic was " burning itself out " in Brooklyn and Richmond.

The advance in new cases was confined to Manhattan, Queens, and the Bronx, where the disease has been most stubborn for several weeks, but the fact that the increase in those boroughs was comparatively moderate tended to support the belief of the authorities that, even there, the epidemic was yielding to control.

In the city as a whole there were 912 new cases in the week ending on July 29, 1,117 in the week ending o' Aug. 5, 1,151 in the week ending on Aug. 12, and 912 in the week ending yesterday.

NEW CASES AND DEATHS

Names and Addresses of the Latest Victims of Paralysis.

The following names and addresses of new cases of infantile paralysis and of deaths were made public yesterday by the Department of Health:

NEW CASES—MANHATTAN.

Sol Grunberg, 167 Orchard St.
Izzie Schivalatt, 162 Stanton St.
Abe Schivalatt, 162 Stanton st.
Lillia Libowitz, 129 Forsyth St.
Julius Malefogel, 70 Orchard St.
John Caichino, 24 Mulberry St.
Marie Moeria, 20 James St.

On the 26th of August, the O'Herlys were going to go home on the 7:12 but as it looked like rain they waited until the afternoon. I took them down very early to get the 4:31. They had to get health certification for the kids & as the two doctors were out they had to wait. I left them waiting. They were very generous & each one gave me 50c making $1.00. That is the biggest tip I ever received.

Bill of Health Certificate – 1916

Much of September was occupied with more farm chores, including rebuilding stone fences *and cutting wood for the winter ahead.* I sawed the big chestnut I had cut down in double lengths. It made a lot of wood. *We worked on the wood for five days.*

On September 24th, I took the milk with the carriage as May, Florrie, and the Aunt had to go to church. We got to church at fifteen minutes after eight & as Mass was not until 9:30 we had started to wait when Mrs. O'Brien rode up & took us for a ride. I hate to go home. If they had given us but a week more it would be all right.

But the next day I was back at Stuyvesant. Everybody was not in school. The Board of Health sent out an order that if anybody was out of the city since Sept. 11 they must stay out of school until called for. This was rather ambiguous. It applied to me as I had been out of the city during that time but it did not apply to me in this respect: that I had not left the city and returned since Sept 11. So the teacher told me to come back.

By November, the Presidential election was the news of the day. On November 4th, I got down to the Garden at about 6:15 and got in line. The doors opened at 7:30 & I got up in the gallery. Then as the balcony was filling slowly I got a seat nearly behind the speaking platform. Predergast was the chairman. Whitman spoke as did Straus. Whitman is a fine speaker, very convincing.

Charles S. Whitman – 1915
Governor of New York

Oscar Solomon Straus
Chairman, NYS Public Service Commission

When Hughes came in the people cheered for 45 minutes. I did not wait for him to finish as I could not hear well and it was getting late. The parade was still going on at 11:00 P.M. as I came out. The Independent *magazine wrote up the Garden speech, reporting that "An audience of fifteen thousand cheered him for more than half an hour and nearly seventy thousand of his partisans worked off their enthusiasm by carrying torches in*

84

a monster parade. Mr. Hughes vindicated the right of American citizens who differed with the President to criticize the foreign policy of the administration."

On the 7th, I went over to hear the returns. At 8:00 the Telegram announced the election of Hughes. I was glad. It seems to be a walkover for Hughes. I got back from there at 11:00 P.M. *But on Wednesday, November 8th, I noted* Things are getting difficult. The *Telegram* announced the election of Wilson at 4 o'clock but of course, false. He is gaining rapidly. The returns were still being shown and I went over. At nine o'clock Wilson had 256 votes to Hughes' 231. I sincerely wish Hughes would get in. I really hate Wilson.

November 10th: It seems that Wilson has been elected which means four more years of misjudgment. This election has clearly demonstrated the inconsistency of the newspapers their guessing and unjustment.

Woodrow Wilson

Charles Evans Hughes

The next day was my birthday. Today I am 17 years old. The time seems to fly as life shortens. The last few years have gone so quickly by. I have been feeling of late that I would like to work but what at I have not the least idea. I am going to study Spanish hard. It may come in useful to me. Went to confession.

Noxon Tombstone – Arden Cemetery

Saturday, May 6, 1916: I am attempting to write a story. Have made good progress so far.

About the Author

Rena Corey holds an M.S. in Secondary Education from C.W. Post. For the past 28 years she has been the proprietor of Mrs. Hudson's Fine Books and Paper, a service specializing in 19th century nonfiction, manuscripts, and ephemera, as well as antiques with unusual graphic interest. Sales are made to historical societies throughout the United States, academic institutions, and individual collectors and dealers. She has been active in the Thomas Wolfe Society as both board member and literary contributor and the Wappingers Historical Society as an archivist.

Her previously published works include articles appearing in *The New York Times, The Poughkeepsie Journal, Southern Dutchess News, Hudson Valley Magazine,* and *The Thomas Wolfe Review*.

CPSIA information can be obtained at www.ICGtesting.com
Printed in the USA
LVOW07s2339030215

425563LV00003B/195/P